QUMRAN

QUMRAN

HANAN ESHEL

A CARTA FIELD GUIDE

2009 First English Edition

Translated from the Hebrew by Ada Yardeni
Edited by Paul King
Managing editor: Barbara L. Ball

ISBN 978-965-220-757-9

Carta books are availabe at special discounts for bulk purchases
for sales promotions, premiums, fund-raising, or educational use.
For details contact:
    Carta, Jerusalem
    18 Ha'uman Street, POB 2500
    Jerusalem 91024, Israel
    E-mail: carta@carta.co.il
    Website: www.holyland-jerusalem.com

Printed in Israel

Contents

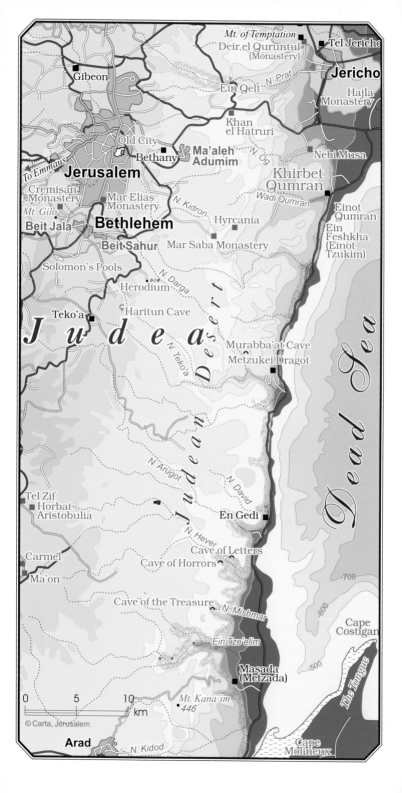

Mt. of Temptation
Deir el Quruntul (Monastery)
Tel Jericho
Gibeon
Ein Qelt
N. Prat
Jericho
Hajla Monastery
Khan el Hatruri
N. Og
Old City
Bethany
Ma'aleh Adumim
Nebi Musa
Jerusalem
Khirbet Qumran
To Emmaus
Cremisan Monastery
Mt. Gilo
Mar Elias Monastery
N. Kidron
Wadi Qumran
Einot Qumran
Beit Jala
Bethlehem
Hyrcania
Ein Feshkha (Einot Tzukim)
Beit Sahur
Mar Saba Monastery
Solomon's Pools
Herodium
N. Darga
J u d e a n   D e s e r t
Teko'a
Haritun Cave
D e a d   S e a
N. Teko'a
Murabba'at Cave
Metzukei Dragot
N. Arugot
N. David
Tel Zif
Horbat Aristobulia
En Gedi
N. Hever
Cave of Letters
Carmel
Cave of Horrors
Ma'on
-700
Cave of the Treasure
N. Mishmar
Cape Costigan
-600
Ein Tze'elim
-500
The Tongue
Masada (Metzada)
0   5   10
km
Mt. Kana'im • 446
© Carta, Jerusalem
Arad
N. Kidod
Cape Molineux

Introduction

General view of Caves 4a and 4b (upper left) from Wadi Qumran.

"The Dead Sea Scrolls are undoubtedly the most important discovery found in Israel in the field of the Bible and history of Judaism and Christianity"—these were the words of Yigael Yadin describing the scrolls found at Khirbet Qumran and the neighboring caves. Fragments of about nine hundred different scrolls from the Second Temple period were discovered in eleven caves at Qumran between 1947 and 1956. Unfortunately, only about twenty scrolls are in fairly good condition, that is, a substantial portion of the scrolls' text survived the ravages of time; the vast majority of material is very fragmentary. At the time that the search for scrolls was carried out, the core area of the Qumran settlement site was also excavated. Today, it houses the visitors' center for the Qumran National Park.

Prof. Yigael Yadin (1917–1984).

Date palms in front of the tower at Khirbet Qumran.

The name Qumran probably derives from the Arabic word *qamar* ("moon") with the dual suffix. One explanation offered for this name is the reflection of the moon in the Dead Sea which, on occasion, appears from the Qumran site as a doublet. During the First and Second Temple periods, this site was called Secacah, likely from the root *s-k-k* ("to cover"), referring to the date-palm leaves used to cover the roofs of the houses. Secacah appears in the list of towns built in the Judean desert during the First Temple period (Joshua 15:61–62).

Every morning, before dawn, the people of Qumran, who called themselves the Yahad, gathered for common prayer. After these daily vespers, each member went to his work: some cultivated date palms at Ein Feshkha, some reared sheep, and others hauled water from Ein Feshkha to Qumran.

There were also members who worked in the community's residential center, preparing the common meals, attending to maintenance matters, and undertaking scribal work on the scrolls. In the late afternoon, the members gathered at the community center, immersed themselves in the ritual pools while reciting certain prayers, and then gathered for the common meal. At sunset, all gathered for the evening prayer. Some members lived on the premises as the local guard contingent, while others

Ein Feshkha.

went to their dwelling caves, which were cut from the Lisan sediment rock, or to tents. (Tents were mainly used during the winter months because of the danger that the caves might collapse after rain.) It seems that members of the Yahad sect were divided into three groups according to their seniority and education, and each group had to study one third of every night. Thus, from evening to dawn, one group or another was awake, studying the scrolls.

The members of the Yahad community, today known as the Qumran sect, were Jews who left Jerusalem and went to live in Qumran on the western shore of the Dead Sea. They developed a unique philosophy and a strict life regimen, which may be discerned from the scrolls and other items found at Qumran.

The two Bedouin shepherds who first discovered the Dead Sea Scrolls.

The Discovery

The first scrolls from Qumran were found in 1947 by two Bedouin shepherds of the Ta'amireh tribe while climbing a rock cliff looking for a lost goat. They noticed a cave, the lower entrance of which was blocked by a stone wall. They saw another entrance above it and threw a stone inside. To their surprise, they heard the sound of the stone hitting a clay vessel. Because it was a difficult climb to the upper entrance and because they lacked means of illumination, the two shepherds did not enter the cave that day.

Two days later, one of the Bedouin shepherds, Muhammad ed-Dibb, entered the

(opposite) Interior of Cave 1. Before 1947 the stone wall partially blocked the entrance.

Kando the antiquities dealer.

The Syrian Orthodox Church of which Kando was a member.

cave alone with an oil lamp. According to him, he found ten cylindrical jars, closed with clay lids. Eight jars were empty and one was filled with what seemed to be the remains of fruit (he emptied it). In the eighth jar he claims to have found three scrolls, two of which were wrapped in cloth. Muhammad removed all ten jars and the three scrolls from the cave. These scrolls were later identified as the complete Isaiah Scroll, the Community Rule and *Pesher Habakkuk* (the Habakkuk Commentary). Some time later, Bedouin digging in the cave found four more scrolls: the second Isaiah Scroll, the War Scroll, the Thanksgiving Scroll, and the Genesis Apocryphon.

The Bedouin shepherds kept the scrolls in their tents for a number of weeks, during which time they showed their findings to various visitors from the clan. Later, they brought the scrolls to Bethlehem in order to try and sell them. However, the antiquities dealers refused to buy them (this was the first time scrolls had been found in the country). They then went to a cobbler, who had a workshop for leather objects, mainly shoes. His name was Khalil Iksander Shahin, nicknamed Kando, and he was a member of the Syrian Orthodox Church. He purchased the scrolls and proceeded to offer them at a good profit to the head of the Syrian Church for the Jerusalem and Bethlehem district, the metropolitan archbishop of Jerusa-

Metropolitan archbishop Mar Athanasius.

lem, Mar Athanasius Yeshua Samuel. The archbishop bought four scrolls for the sum of 24 Palestinian pounds (equivalent to 110 dollars). The other three scrolls were acquired by Eliezer Lippa Sukenik (father of Yigael Yadin) with money from the Hebrew University of Jerusalem. On Saturday, 29 November 1947, Sukenik went to Bethlehem and purchased both the War Scroll and the Thanksgiving Scroll for 35 Palestinian pounds. A month later he also acquired the second Isaiah Scroll.

One of the two jars purchased by Prof. Sukenik, now on display in the Israel Museum.

In the meantime, initial military clashes took place in Jerusalem between Jews and Arabs, which escalated into the Israel War of Independence. In mid-February 1948 Mar Athanasius submitted the three scrolls, which the Bedouin shepherd had found inside the jar, to the American Schools of Oriental Research (ASOR) in Jerusalem, north of Damascus Gate. In 1948, three American scholars—Prof. Millar Burrows from Yale University and two young research fellows who had recently completed their Ph.D. dissertations, William H. Brownlee and John C. Trever—had intended to spend the academic year at the school. With the mounting hostilities, two of the scholars left Jerusalem and only Trever remained at the school. He examined the scrolls, recognized their importance, and photographed three of them (the Archbishop prohibited the opening of the Genesis Apocryphon scroll because of its brittle state).

Trever and two other American scholars, who were called back from Amman to Jerusalem because of the importance of the findings, persuaded the metropolitan to remove the scrolls from Jerusalem and take them for safekeeping to the United States. At the end of March 1948, the metropolitan archbishop left for New York with four

William H. Brownlee (1917–1983) holding the Community Rule scroll.

scrolls: the complete Isaiah manuscript, the Community Rule, the Habakkuk Commentary, and the Genesis Apocryphon. He tried to sell the scrolls in the United States but no one would buy them. There were two reasons for this. In the meantime, contents of the first of the three scrolls had been published by the three Americans. Trever had photographed the scrolls' con-

John C. Trever (1915–2006) photographing the Community Rule scroll.

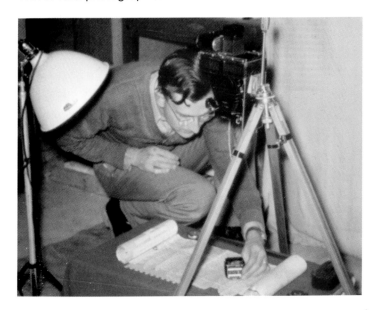

Ad appearing in The Wall Street Journal, 1 June 1954.

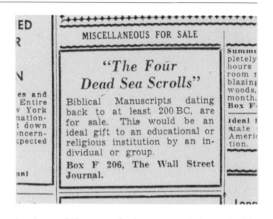

tents and these scholars were interested in the contents of the scrolls rather than the scrolls themselves. The second reason was the unclear legal state of the scrolls. Potential buyers avoided purchasing them for fear that they might be ordered by the courts to return them to the Middle East. On 1 June 1954, the Metropolitan placed an announcement in *The Wall Street Journal* that these Dead Sea Scrolls were for sale. Yigael Yadin, who at that time was visiting the United States, reacted quickly and

Interior and exterior of the Shrine of the Book in Jerusalem where the Dead Sea Scrolls are presently housed.

acquired the four scrolls for the State of Israel. He paid 250,000 American dollars. In this way, the seven scrolls (the three bought by Sukenik and the four scrolls bought by Yadin), which were discovered by the Bedouins in 1947, reached western Jerusalem, now a part of the State of Israel. In 1965, the Shrine of the Book was built on the premises of the Israel Museum in Jerusalem for the express purpose of displaying these scrolls.

Cave 1 where the first scrolls were found.

The First Seven Scrolls

The seven scrolls discovered by the Bedouin in Cave 1 at Qumran in 1947 reflect the nature of the "library" discovered at the site. These scrolls, as well as additional scroll finds, may be divided into three groups: (a) biblical scrolls; (b) sectarian scrolls; and (c) other scrolls.

In Cave 1, Bedouin found two manuscripts from the Book of Isaiah. The first one, called "the complete Isaiah manu-

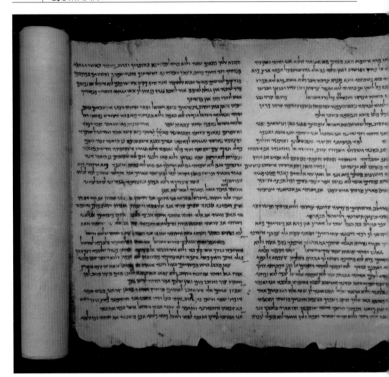

The Great Isaiah Scroll and detail (below).

script," is 7.34 meters long and contains the entire Book of Isaiah, chapters 1 to 66. The other manuscript, the so-called "second Isaiah Scroll," is fragmentary. The texts of the two scrolls differ in style. The text of the complete manuscript is coarser, the scribe being less pedantic concerning the spelling, adding specific letters to indicate how words should be pronounced (*matres lectiones*), exchanging difficult words for more common ones, and sometimes integrating Aramaic words into the text. The scribe of the second Isaiah scroll copied the original text at hand almost verbatim, and this scroll is very close to the Masoretic text.

The first seven scrolls include four sectarian scrolls. The Habakkuk Commentary reflects a unique practice of exegesis developed among the members of the Qumran sect. In this exegetical form, the author cites a verse, followed by the words "Its true interpretation is" (Heb. *pesher ha-davar al* or *pishro al*), and then he interprets the verse as describing events in his own time. The Qumran sect members believed that they lived in the End of Days, and tried to prove in their commentaries that most of the prophecies were realized in the last generation, except for the imminent Day of Judgment.

The so-called "second Isaiah Scroll."

Historical figures played a part in the events described in the Commentaries, but the commentators avoided indicating their names. It is unclear if this was because they feared that the rulers in Judea, who were attacked in the Commentaries, would harm them, or, perhaps because they tried to prevent unauthorized people (i.e., those who were not members of the sect) from understanding historical allusions appearing in the scrolls. The leader of the Yahad community is referred to in the Commentaries as the "Teacher of Righteousness." His opponent, who was also a religious leader, is called in the Commentaries the "Man of the Lie." The political leader who tried to kill the Teacher of Righteousness is called the "Wicked Priest." The Habakkuk Commentary is the best preserved of all the com-

The Habakkuk Commentary.

mentaries found in Qumran, and therefore it is of utmost importance for any historical study of the sect. The commentator avoids using the name of God, except when citing explicit names from the Bible. In these cases, the name of God is written in Hebrew letters, which developed in Judah

The Habakkuk Commentary (detail). The words marked in red read "YHWH," the name of God, in Hebrew script.

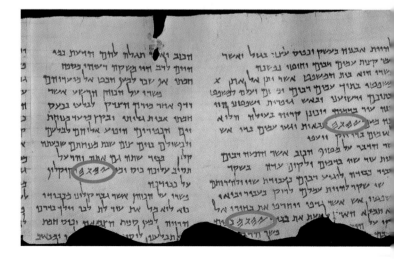

from the ancient Hebrew script prevailing in the First Temple period, whereas the rest of the scrolls display the local "Jewish" script, which evolved from the Aramaic script in the Second Temple period.

Another sectarian scroll is the Community Rule, the first and main part of which is *Serekh haYahad* (the Manual of Discipline). It includes the laws which the disciples of the Teacher of Righteousness accepted when they joined the Yahad community and took the oath of fidelity. The word *serekh* in the Qumran lexicon means "rule," and this scroll is the "book of rules" of the community. It describes, *inter alia*, the procedure of becoming a member of the community. The procedure took two years. When a person asked to join the community, an overseer, who was responsible for the spiritual and financial aspects of the sect, interviewed him and decided whether he was ready to begin the process of joining the group. During the first year, that is, during the months between the arrival of the candidate and Pentecost—the feast in which the members of the community swore to keep the laws of God—the candidate was allowed to hold his personal belongings. When the feast arrived, the yearly ceremony took place, in which the members took an oath of fidelity to the community and the laws of God. If the candidate received approval in the first vote, he was allowed to add his property

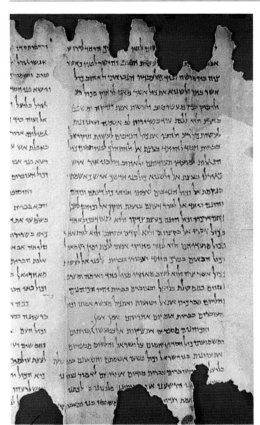

The Community Rule.

to that of the community. At this stage, the overseer prepared an account of the candidate's assets. This account was used in case the candidate failed to be accepted by the community at the end of the second year, or if he decided to leave the community during this second year. If the majority decided to accept the candidate in the second voting, which took place before Pentacost of the second year, he had to take an oath of fidelity and then became a full member of the community. At this stage, if the new member decided to leave the sect,

Imaginary portrait of Philo of Alexandria from the Middle Ages.

his property was not returned to him.

The Manual of Discipline, which comprises most of the Community Rule, describes in detail the punishments for transgressing the community rules—expulsion from the common meals for different periods of time. Thus, for example, a member who lied was expelled for six months; a member who bore a grudge against another member was punished for six months, and

The Community Rule.

whoever interrupted the speech of another member was expelled from the common meal for ten days. A member who defamed his fellow member was expelled for a whole year, and whoever defamed the community was expelled from the community forever. The Manual of Discipline listed in detail the roles of the members, giving a detailed picture of their daily life. They had to dedicate one third of the night to learning, "all nights of the year, read the Book and seek justice." The rules of the Yahad community resemble the way of life of the Essenes as described by Philo of Alexandria and Jose-

Imaginary portrait of Pliny the Elder from the Middle Ages.

The War Scroll.

phus Flavius. According to Pliny the Elder, the Essenes lived on the western shore of the Dead Sea, leading most scholars to aver that the Qumran community should be identified with one of the Essene groups.

The War Scroll, also known as the Scroll of the War between the Sons of Light and the Sons of Darkness, is a sectarian composition describing the war preceding the Day of the Lord. This war would continue for forty-nine years, and is divided into peri-

ods of seven years each. In the sabbatical (seventh) year a ceasefire would come into force. Toward the end of the war, the angels would join the Sons of Light and help them to overcome the Sons of Darkness. The scroll discusses many issues, including military tactics of the Sons of Light (partly influenced by Greco-Roman war doctrine), the kinds of war trumpets and the various battle sounds they produce, the rules concerning the Temple service during the (peaceful) sabbatical year, detailed descriptions of the angels who will help the Sons of Light in their war, and the prayers and hymns that should be recited during the war.

The Thanksgiving Scroll also belongs to the sectarian scrolls. It includes about forty hymns not previously known. These psalms begin with the words "Thank Thee my Lord" or "Thank Thee my God." The hymns in the Thanksgiving Scroll are divided into personal hymns, called the Teacher's Hymns by Qumran scholars, on the assumption that they were composed by the Teacher of Righteousness, and public hymns, called the Community Hymns. In some of the hymns classified as the Teacher's Hymns

The Thanksgiving Scroll (detail).

Prof. Sukenik examining the Thanksgiving Scroll.

the composer told of his personal troubles, of his failures and successes, and of his struggle with his enemies. In certain chapters, the composer expounds in astounding superlatives on his greatness, and a few lines later describes himself as a complete failure. Linguistically, the Thanksgiving Scroll is, no doubt, the most beautiful of all the Qumran scrolls.

The Genesis Apocryphon was found by Bedouin in Cave 1. Unlike the other scrolls from this cave which were in Hebrew, this one was written in Aramaic. Since it does not include any typical sectarian expressions, scholars did not ascribe its composition to a member of the Yahad community. The composer of this scroll expanded the text of Genesis in an exegetical way, which in general reflects the nature of the Jewish literary work of the Second Temple

The unopened Genesis Apocryphon.

period. Some of the exegetical expansions in this scroll later appear in the Talmudic legends (Midrash). Below are three examples of the exegetical additions appearing in the Genesis Apocryphon:

The first example concerns the question of explaining the verses in which Abraham asked Sarah to lie to Pharaoh and present herself as Abraham's sister, thus causing Pharaoh to take a married woman. The composer of the Genesis Apocryphon explained that the night before Abraham's voyage to Egypt God warned him in a dream that he may be killed because of his (beautiful) wife. Hence, Abraham asked his wife to lie to Pharaoh in order to save his own life. The second example is based on verses in Genesis which prove that Sarah was over sixty-five years old when Pharaoh took her to his palace. This caused the composer of the Genesis Apocryphon to add a descrip-

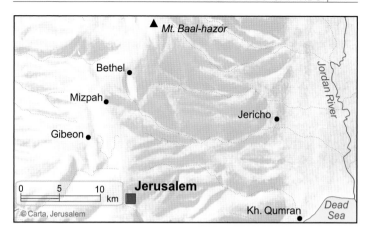

Map showing proximity of Mt. Baal-hazor to Bethel.

tion praising Sarah's beauty, and explaining why Pharaoh desired her despite her old age. The third example concerns a geographical problem—the composer knew that from Bethel there is no view of "west and east, north and south" and therefore he wrote that God asked Abraham to climb to "the mount Hazor, left of Bethel." Mount Baal-hazor, 1,006 meters high, is located about three miles north of Bethel, and from there is a view of most of the country. According to the composer of the scroll this was the site where Abraham saw the land of Canaan and received the Lord's promise that his descendants will inherit it.

More Caves & Finds

The archaeological research could not be continued until the end of the War of Independence. In 1949, a UN officer of Belgian origin, accompanied by an offi-

cer of the Jordanian army, determined the whereabouts of the cave in which the first seven scrolls had been found. Following this discovery, authorized archaeological excavations commenced at Qumran. The first cave was explored by the Jordanian Department of Antiquities in collaboration with French archaeologists from the École Biblique et Archéologique (founded in 1890 by the French Dominican order), situated north of the Damascus Gate in Jerusalem. In the cave, the excavators found fragments of about seventy different scrolls, including fragments of the seven scrolls earlier found in this cave.

(opposite) Storage jar found at Khirbet Qumran resembling those discovered in Cave 1.

Since the jars found in the ruins of Qumran were identical to those found by the Bedouin in the cave, the French archaeologists started to excavate the site in 1951. Over the next six years, annual excavations took place, conducted by the Dominican Father Roland de Vaux.

Roland de Vaux.

In late 1951, the Bedouin brought documents different from those found at Qumran to the markets of Bethlehem and East Jerusalem. Unlike the literary texts

(above) Coin from the Bar Kokhba period inscribed "of the freedom of Jerusalem."

(right) The caves used by the Bar Kokhba fighters.

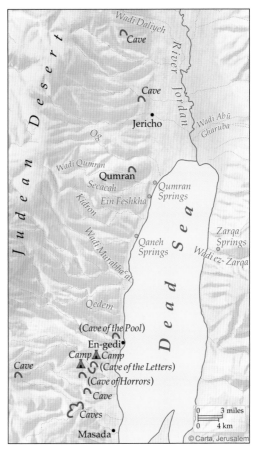

from Qumran, these were documentary texts from the time of the Bar Kokhba revolt (132–136 CE). According to the Bedouin, these documents were found in the caves of Wadi Murabbaʿat (near the cliffs of Wadi Darajeh). In 1952, following this discovery, the archaeologists conducted excavations in four caves located on the northern side of Wadi Murabbaʿat. Here they found about 170 documents, most of them from the time of the Bar Kokhba revolt. In the meantime, the Bedouin returned to Qumran and found another cave in the limestone cliff south of the first cave. In this second cave (listed as Cave 2), fragments of thirty-three different scrolls were discovered, among them small fragments from the Book of Sirach (*Ecclesiasticus*). In about 180 BCE, Jesus son of Sirach, an author from Jerusalem, wrote a book containing fifty chapters which resembles the Book of Proverbs.

Following the discovery by the Bedouin of the two first caves, archaeologists concluded that more caves might exist. They decided to explore the calcareous cliff in the region between Kibbutz Almog and Ein Feshkha. In this survey of March to April 1952, 250 caves were explored, but additional scroll fragments were found in only one collapsed cave. The findings consisted of fragments from fourteen different scrolls and one complete scroll whose text was incised in three copper sheets.

The Copper Scroll was found "open," that is, divided into two rolls. One roll

The Copper Scroll at the time of discovery in Cave 3.

Prof. James Baker sawing a segment of the Copper Scroll.

contained a third of the text and the other the remaining two thirds.

Although found in 1952, the decision how to open it was not taken until 1956. Because the copper sheets were dry, it was clear that any attempt to unroll them would cause their disintegration. The scroll was sent to Manchester, England, and there a fine-toothed saw used for operating on the human skull was used to cut the copper.

Detailed replica of the Copper Scroll.

The incised text of the scroll describes sixty-three treasure troves hidden in various places in the region of Jerusalem and the northern part of the Judean desert. The description includes a list of items contained in each trove. The sums of silver and gold recorded in the Copper Scroll

are enormous and impressive even for to-day's standards: 4,630 silver and gold talents (total weight of more than 115,750 kg), 65 gold ingots, 619 silver and gold vessels, 608 clay vessels containing coins, as well as additional treasures. Shortly after the Copper Scroll was opened, the government of Jordan gave John Allegro, one of the scroll scholars, permission to search for these treasures. A team headed by Allegro excavated various sites mentioned in the Copper Scroll but no treasure was found. Scholars still do not agree whether the treasure trove descriptions are genuine or fictional accounts. Those who believe that the treasures really did exist rely on the fact that the description of the hiding

Scholar examining sections of the Copper Scroll.

The unrolled Copper Scroll.

Cave 3 in which the Copper Scroll was found.

places is real and detailed. Their opponents claim that the huge sums prove that it is an imaginative description. The discovery of the Copper Scroll stimulated the imagination of romantic minds and people began to show interest in the Qumran scrolls. Adventurers excavated in Qumran and other sites in the Judean Desert trying to find the hidden treasures. The ancient name of Qumran—Secacah—appears in the Copper Scroll. Some of the treasures described in the scroll were hidden in its vicinity. The route from Jericho to Secacah and a dam in the nearby stream are also described in the scroll.

In March 1952, the archaeologists returned to East Jerusalem rejoicing at their success in discovering Cave 3 before the Bedouin reached it. This success was short-lived. The first three caves that were discovered are in the limestone cliffs. In the summer of 1952, Bedouins discovered scroll fragments in another cave, located below the aqueduct, which drew water from Wadi Qumran to the site. This cave is very close to the marl terrace on which Khirbet Qumran is located.

Following the discovery of the new cave, the Bedouin started searching for caves on the marl terrace. In August 1952, they found two small artificial caves west of the site, which contained more than 16,000 scroll fragments. These fragments were found in the dust, which penetrated the caves after the Second Temple period, and the Bedouin sifted it skillfully. In September 1952, the first fragments from the new caves reached the antiquities markets in Bethlehem and East Jerusalem. Quarrels among the Bedouin who searched the cave led the French archaeologists swiftly to the new caves. In the eastern cave they found about one thousand fragments (most of them from a Hebrew version of the Book of Samuel that resembled the text of the Septuagint). Only these fragments survived out of the 16,000

An extra-canonical edition to the Book of Samuel following 1 Sam 20:27 (4QSam^a col. 10, lines 6–9).

fragments found in the two caves. Roland de Vaux, who was the first scholar to enter the eastern cave, claimed that the first damage to the hidden scrolls was caused by Roman soldiers who entered the cave and cut the scrolls into small pieces with their sword. In this way, de Vaux explained the fact that parts of the fragments were cut in straight lines. Damage was caused, according to his explanation, by moths and weather conditions. Father Jozef Milik, who

*From left to right,
the openings of
caves 4b, 4a and 5.*

dedicated most of his life researching the fragments from Cave 4, claimed that the damage to the scrolls was natural. Since there was no way to distinguish between the fragments coming from the somewhat larger eastern cave and those coming from the western cave, the former was called Cave 4a and the latter Cave 4b.

The archaeologists found an additional cave north of the larger one (4a) and called it Cave 5. In this cave, fragments of twenty-

Cave 6 with Wadi Qumran in background.

five scrolls were found, most of them biblical, and a fragment of the Damascus Covenant scroll. Later, the Bedouin guided the excavators to the cave, which was discovered before Caves 4a and 4b. This cave is now called Cave 6. The Bedouin brought out of this cave fragments from thirty-one different scrolls, most of them written on papyrus. In this cave, more fragments of the Damascus Document were found.

The Damascus Document was known *before* the discovery of the first scrolls in Cave 1. Two copies of this work had been found in the Cairo Genizah. The document is mainly a collection of sectarian rules interwoven with the history of the sect. It contains recognized nicknames appearing in the Commentaries. Since, according to the Damascus Document, marriage and private property were allowed, most schol-

UNIV. LIB. CAMB. T-S 10 K 6

וְעַתָּה שִׁמְעוּ כֹּל יוֹדְעֵי צֶדֶק וּבִינוּ בְּמַעֲשֵׂי
אֵל כִּי רִיב לוֹ עִם כָּל בָּשָׂר וּמִשְׁפָּט יַעֲשֶׂה בְּכָל מְנָאֲצָיו
כִּי בְּמׇעֳלָם אֲשֶׁר עֲזָבוּהוּ הִסְתִּיר פָּנָיו מִיִּשְׂרָאֵל וּמִמִּקְדָּשׁוֹ
וַיִּתְּנֵם לְחֶרֶב וּבְזׇכְרוֹ בְּרִית רִאשֹׁנִים הִשְׁאִיר שְׁאֵרִית
לְיִשְׂרָאֵל וְלֹא נְתָנָם לְכָלָה וּבְקֵץ חָרוֹן שָׁנִים שָׁלֹשׁ מֵאוֹת
וְתִשְׁעִים לְתִתּוֹ אוֹתָם בְּיַד נְבוּכַדְנֶאצַּר מֶלֶךְ בָּבֶל
פְּקָדָם וַיַּצְמַח מִיִּשְׂרָאֵל וּמֵאַהֲרֹן שׁוֹרֶשׁ מַטַּעַת לִירֹשׁ
אֶת אַרְצוֹ וְלִדְשֹׁן בְּטוּב אַדְמָתוֹ וַיָּבִינוּ בַּעֲוֹנָם וַיֵּדְעוּ כִּי
אֲנָשִׁים אֲשֵׁמִים הֵם וַיִּהְיוּ כְּעִוְרִים וְכִמְגַשְׁשִׁים דֶּרֶךְ
שָׁנִים עֶשְׂרִים וַיָּבֶן אֵל אֶל מַעֲשֵׂיהֶם כִּי בְּלֵב שָׁלֵם דְּרָשׁוּהוּ
וַיָּקֶם לָהֶם מוֹרֵה צֶדֶק לְהַדְרִיכָם בְּדֶרֶךְ לִבּוֹ וַיּוֹדַע
לְדוֹרוֹת אַחֲרוֹנִים אֵת אֲשֶׁר עָשָׂה בְּדוֹר אַחֲרוֹן בַּעֲדַת בּוֹגְדִים
הֵם סָרֵי דֶרֶךְ הִיא הָעֵת אֲשֶׁר הָיָה כָּתוּב עָלֶיהָ כְּפָרָה סוֹרֵרָה
כֵּן סָרַר יִשְׂרָאֵל בַּעֲמוֹד אִישׁ הַלָּצוֹן אֲשֶׁר הִטִּיף לְיִשְׂרָאֵל
מֵימֵי כָזָב וַיַּתְעֵם בְּתֹהוּ לֹא דֶרֶךְ לְהָשַׁח גַּבְהוּת עוֹלָם וְלָסוּר
מִנְּתִיבוֹת צֶדֶק וְלָסִיעַ גְּבוּל אֲשֶׁר גָּבְלוּ רִאשֹׁנִים בְּנַחֲלָתָם לְמַעַן
הַדְבֵּק בָּהֶם אֵת אָלוֹת בְּרִיתוֹ לְהַסְגִּירָם לְחֶרֶב נֹקֶמֶת נְקַם
בְּרִית בַּעֲבוּר אֲשֶׁר דָּרְשׁוּ בַּחֲלָקוֹת וַיִּבְחֲרוּ בְּמַהֲתַלּוֹת וַיְצַפּוּ
לִפְרָצוֹת וַיִּבְחֲרוּ בְּטוֹב הַצַּוָּאר וַיַּצְדִּיקוּ רָשָׁע וַיַּרְשִׁיעוּ צַדִּיק
וַיַּעַבְרוּ בְּרִית וַיָּפֵרוּ חוֹק וַיָּגוֹדּוּ עַל נֶפֶשׁ צַדִּיק וְכֹל הוֹלְכֵי
תָמִים תִּעֲבָה נַפְשָׁם וַיִּרְדְּפוּם לְחֶרֶב וַיָּסִיסוּ לְרִיב עָם וַיִּחַר אַף

ars assumed that the rules appearing in this document were fixed for the disciples of the Teacher of Righteousness, who lived in "camps," and did not join the community residing in Qumran. Solomon Schechter, who discovered the Cairo Genizah, published the pages of the Genizah Damascus Document under the name Zadokite Fragments. When Sukenik started to study the scrolls he acquired in November 1947, he noticed the similarity between these scrolls, especially the War Scroll, and the

Page from the Damascus Document (Cambridge University Library T-S 10K6) discovered in the Cairo Genizah.

Solomon Schechter at work in Cambridge University Library, 1898.

work from the Cairo Genizah. The discovery of the Damascus Document in Caves 4, 5 and 6 pointed to the origin of this composition. It seems that the disciples of the Teacher of Righteousness were divided into groups, some of which permitted marriage and private property, while others followed an ascetic way of life, sharing their property and living according to the rules appearing in the Community Rule.

The two copies of the Damascus Document from the Cairo Genizah were copied in the ninth and tenth centuries CE, and therefore it is reasonable to relate them to rumors in the late eighth or the early ninth century about the discovery of caves near

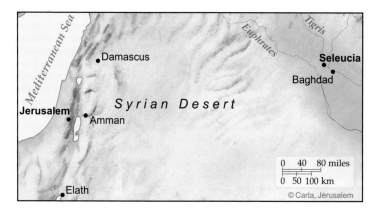

Location of Seleucia where Timotheus I served as patriarch.

Jericho. In a letter written in Syriac (Christian Aramaic) by Timotheus I (726–819), the patriarch of Seleucia (located near Baghdad), he tells of Jews who wanted to convert to Christianity, and informed him that ten years earlier books were found in a cave near Jericho. According to their story, an Arab hunter who chased his dog into a cave discovered those books. When this became known to the Jews in Jerusalem many of them hurried in search of the cave and found biblical books there, as well as other books in Hebrew. One of the Jews told Timotheus that more that 200 psalms appear in these books, while the Book of Psalms contains only 150. Timotheus wrote to Christian priests in Palestine asking them to find these books for him. It is possible that copies of the Damascus Document from the cave near Qumran, found in the days of Timotheus, were copied in Jerusalem and finally found their way to the Cairo Genizah.

Father Milik examining the scroll fragments from Cave 4 in the Rockefeller Museum.

The Rockefeller Museum in Jerusalem.

The Scrolls Found in Cave 4

When Caves 4a and 4b were discovered and it became known that the Bedouin were in possession of more than ten thousand scroll fragments found in them, the Jordanian Department of Antiquities realized that it faced two initial problems. In the first place, the Dominican scholars of the French École Biblique et Archéologique were not able to cope with such an abundance of material. The second problem was lack of a budget. Since no one knew how many fragments were held by the Bedouin, it was impossible to fix the budget for their acquisition. In addition, there was the possibility that material would be smuggled abroad and fragments belonging to a single scroll would be separated and circulate independently. Unauthorized archaeological

excavation is illegal, and therefore the Bedouin did not bring
their finds directly to the Rockefeller Museum. Kando, the dealer who acquired the first scrolls
found in Cave 1, was the agent
who bought the fragments from
the Bedouin and delivered them
to the museum. The Jordanians
and the curators of the Rockefeller Museum fixed the price
for all the fragments—one Jordanian Dinar (then equivalent to

*Carefully unrolling
a scroll fragment
from Cave 4 for
examination.*

one Pound Sterling) for each written square
centimeter (the Bedouin did not receive any
payment for the unwritten margins of the
scrolls). In order to prevent the scrolls from
being torn into small fragments and divided
equally among the Bedouin who had discovered them, the Jordanians decided to
pay one Dinar and 10 piasters for a fragment larger than 10 cubic cm, and an additional 10 piasters for a fragment larger than
20 cubic cm, and so forth. The larger the
fragment, the greater would be their value.

*Scroll fragments
from Cave 4
as brought to
the Rockefeller
Museum.*

By creating these fi-
nancial conditions for
parchment purchases,
the Bedouin would not
be encouraged to tear
the scrolls into small
fragments. The process
of acquiring the scroll

The "Scrollery" in the Rockefeller Museum with Dr. Hunziger.

fragments from the Bedouin continued until July 1958.

In 1953, in order to solve the problem of financing the publication of the scrolls, the Jordanians established an international committee consisting of eight scholars (from the United States and Britain [two scholars each] and from Poland, France, Switzerland and Germany [one scholar each]). Their task was twofold: scientific and administrative. They were asked to clean the fragments, identify them, try to join them into larger pieces, and finally publish them. In addition, they were asked to find funding for purchasing additional fragments from

The international committee gathered at the Rockefeller Museum. Seated facing the camera, from left to right, Frs. Milik, de Vaux and Starcky.

the Bedouin. The Jordanians promised to give the scrolls, after their publication, to every institute that would donate money for this purpose. Following this promise, a number of academic institutions contributed money to the Rockefeller Museum for the acquisition of the fragments from Caves 4a and 4b. These institutions were McGill University (Canada), the University of Manchester (England), Heidelberg University (Germany), the Vatican Library, the McCormick Theological Seminary (Chicago), and All Souls' Church (New York). The publication of the fragments took much longer than expected (the last fragments from Cave 4 were only published in 2001). All scrolls discovered and purchased between 1949 and 1956 were kept in the Rockefeller Museum, which at that time was under the manage-

Dr. Hunziger examining one of the scrolls.

Jozef Milik (left) and John Strugnell in the room in the Rockefeller Museum where the fragments from Cave 4 were identified and arranged.

(left to right) Frank Cross, Jozef Milik and John Strugnell examining scroll fragments.

ment of an international board. In July 1960, the Jordanian government placed a ban on moving the Qumran fragments abroad, and offered to return the money donated by academic institutions for their purchase. This decision put an end to the hope of these institutions acquiring the scrolls.

About 16,000 written fragments, originally belonging to about 600 different scrolls, have been found in Caves 4a and 4b. In average this would yield about 30 fragments for each scroll, but in fact there are scrolls of which only a single fragment survives and other scrolls in which about 250 fragments have survived. Cave 4 yielded scrolls in three languages (Hebrew, Aramaic and Greek), and four different scripts ("Jewish," Paleo-Hebrew, Greek, and a cryptic script comprising Hebrew and Greek letters in mirror image, written from left to right). In general, there is a similarity between the sectarian scrolls found in Cave 1 and the fragments of Cave 4 in that copies of similar compositions of all the sectarian scrolls found in Cave 1 have been discovered also in Cave 4. For example, copies of the Community Rule, the War Scroll, the Thanksgiving Scroll and the Commentaries (*Pesharim*) were found in both caves.

In Cave 4, 118 Hebrew scrolls were discovered which included fragments from the entire canon of the Old Testament, except for Esther. Among the most important findings were "early" fragments, such as those from the Book of Exodus, copied around the mid-third century BCE, and portions from Samuel and Jeremiah, copied in c. 200 BCE, that is, much earlier than the establishment of the settlement at Qumran. How, then, did these scrolls arrive at Qumran? It is quite probable that these scrolls belonged to earlier generations of one or more members who settled in Qumran at a later date.

Among the scroll fragments from Cave 4 are 20 sheets of *tefillin* (phylacteries) and 7 sheets of mezuzahs (a small case containing brief portions from the Pentateuch which are attached to the doorpost of doors and entryways). In addition, Hebrew and Aramaic frag-

(right, above) Tefillin *(phylactery) fragment from Qumran; (right) the open capsule bought by Yigael Yadin (cave unknown) with inscribed parchment slips inside.*

Fragments of the Book of Enoch from Cave 4.

Sundial found at Khirbet Qumran.

ments of various apocryphal compositions have been found: the Books of Enoch, the Book of Jubilees, the Book of Tobit, the Testament of Levi and the Testament of Naphtali. Among the sectarian compositions found in Cave 4 there are eight copies of the Damascus Document, as well as large and important fragments of Qumranic wisdom literature, many fragments dealing with the solar calendar and passages pertaining to the priestly service allotments at the Temple in Jerusalem.

A very important sectarian composition which has drawn much attention is a halakhic letter called *Miqtsat Ma'asei ha-Torah* ("Selection of the Works of the Law"), known by its acronym MMT, six copies of which were found in Cave 4. This letter was written by the head of the Qumran sect to one of his opponents, discussing in detail more than twenty religious rules (*halakhot*) for which he held a stricter position than

Fragments of the so-called MMT scroll from Cave 4.

that of the addressee. This letter is significant for an understanding of the Halakha of the sect members and for clarifying their history. It is possible that this was the letter sent by the Teacher of Righteousness to the Wicked Priest mentioned in one of the Commentaries.

Khirbet Qumran: The Community Center

An aqueduct, starting below one of the falls in Wadi Qumran, led to Khirbet Qumran. A dam was built under the waterfall (described in the Copper Scroll as "a large stone heap in the ravine of Secacah"). This dam diverted part of the floodwaters to the aqueduct, which also collected rainwater from the cliff. A hewn tunnel led the aqueduct northward, out of Wadi Qumran. The

The aqueduct on the limestone cliff.

aqueduct was hedged by support walls, and stones covered it to prevent it being filled with mud by flash floods. The aqueduct passed above Cave 6, and arriving on the plain, west of the site, it became an open channel. Today, one can see the open channel, which conducted water from the cliff to the site. The floodwaters were important in that they met the requirements for purification rituals. The many ritual baths (*miqva'ot*) filled by the aqueduct occupied about 17 percent of the site area.

It seems that three factors led to the choice of Qumran as the center of the Yahad sect: (a) The nearby springs of Ein Feshkha provided the people of Qumran with drinking and cooking water, and was used for the irrigation of the palm trees that grew near the springs. Date palms and beets were

(opposite) The aqueduct on the marl plain (above) which conducted water from the cliff to the aqueduct at Khirbet Qumran (below).

the only plants that could survive the relatively high saline count of the fresh-water springs. (b) The location of Qumran as the terminal point of routes from the Judean Hills in the west or from the Jordan River Valley in the north, made it, in effect, a "dead end"; this appealed to people who wanted to seclude themselves in the barren wilderness. During the period of the Second Temple, the Dead Sea level was higher than today and the waters

The cliffs south of Ein Feshkha.

Scroll jar from Khirbet Qumran similar to those found in Cave 1.

reached the base of the cliffs south of Ein Feshkha. Only in recent years has the sea level begun to drop significantly. Walking from the northern end of the Dead Sea to its southern area was difficult in those days and most people who wanted to go from Jericho to Ein Gedi and to Masada traveled by boat. Thus, people reaching Qumran from different directions in the Judean desert did not arrive there by chance. (c) The flash floods, which swept through Wadi Qumran a few times each winter, supplied water for the ritual baths built at the site.

Official excavations at Khirbet Qumran began in 1951 in order to assist in the dating of the scrolls discovered in Cave 1. Gradually, the archaeological dig was expanded and after six seasons most of the site had been excavated. The last on-site expedition, conducted by Roland de Vaux, was in 1956. The excavations revealed that there were three periods of settlement at the site: the late Israelite period (Iron Age II), the Second Temple period, and the short duration during the Bar Kokhba revolt.

The first detected settlement at Qumran was in the eighth century BCE and apparently continued until nearly the end of the First Temple period, in 586 BCE. During this time, a rectangular stronghold was built at the site. On its eastern side were residential quarters and on its western side an oval water cistern. This cistern is the only remnant from the First Temple period. In Khirbet Qumran, two jar handles were found with stamps marked "to the king" (lamelekh), which are dated from 705 to 701 BCE, the time of the revolt of Hezekiah, king of Judah, against Sennacherib, king of Assyria. The name of the site—Secacah—appears in Joshua 15:61. The stronghold was de-

Jar handles stamped with royal lamelekh ("to the king") seals were found throughout Judea. This one is from Hebron.

The cistern (in center) from the First Temple period.

stroyed at the beginning of the sixth century BCE, close to the time of the destruction of the First Temple. The site was abandoned for a long period until the Yahad members settled here in the late second century BCE.

Most of the remnants found in Qumran date from the Second Temple period. After the Romans conquered the site in 68 CE, a Roman guard camp was stationed there until the fall of Masada in 73 or 74 CE. During the Bar Kokhba revolt (132–136 CE), a number of Jewish soldiers stayed at the site, possibly overlooking approaches from the north. An oil lamp containing coins from the Bar Kokhba period was discovered in the ruins of the tower at the northwest corner of the eastern building.

De Vaux found 1,223 coins at Qumran dating from the Hellenistic and Roman periods. On the basis of these findings, he determined the settlement chronology of the site. The group, which resided in Qumran, was, no doubt, wealthy. In the Commentaries we find that during the hard drought

Oil lamp from Qumran, Herodian period. Traces of a palm-fiber wick were found in the lamp's nozzle

and famine in Judea in 63 BCE, when Honi the Circle-maker brought the much needed rain, people joined the group at Qumran not because of their belief in the Teacher of Righteousness, but only to survive the famine. It appears that the people of Qumran ate meat and drank wine in their daily common meals, and one may assume that, living in the desert, they were less stricken by the drought than the farmers in Judea.

The many coins, as well as the glass vessels and other finds at the site, testify to the prosperity of the group residing in Qumran in the Second Temple period. From the coins we learn that the site had been rebuilt in the second century BCE after being abandoned for about 500 years. The archaeological layer dating from its settlement in the second century BCE to the earthquake of 31 BCE, was named phase I by de Vaux. Since two stages were observed in this layer, he named them phase Ia and phase Ib. In the early phase (Ia), the building from the time of the Iron Age was restored and the round cistern was cleaned and re-plastered. In the later phase (Ib), two buildings were built at the site: an eastern, cubic building and a western structure built around the round cistern. The finds from the various buildings indicate that the western structure served as the administrative center whereas the eastern building was the public center of the community. After the earthquake of 31

The hoard of silver coins found at Qumran was almost entirely of Tyrian tetradrachmas, like the one shown here. On obverse, head of the Phoenician god Melqart, and on reverse, an Egyptian-style eagle on a ship's prow (referring to Tyre's port).

Remains of the tower at the northwest corner of the eastern building.

BCE, the site was rebuilt. This layer, which was named phase II by de Vaux, existed until the Roman conquest in 68 CE. De Vaux surmised that following the earthquake the site was abandoned for about thirty years and then resettled early in the first century CE, after Herod's death. However, recent archaeological evidence indicates that the site was continuously settled and that there was no gap in human presence during the thirty years after the earthquake, except for a very brief intermission when fire destroyed the place in 4 BCE. This fire seems to have been the result of tumults in Judea after Herod's death.

No scrolls were found inside the buildings at Qumran and this raises the question of the precise function of the various rooms. The following account contains data concerning the finds from the archaeological excavations in Qumran together with written documentation about life in Qumran as described in the Scroll of the Community Rule, the Damascus Document and the description of the Essenes provided by Josephus. The combination of archaeological finds and textual evidence may enable us to offer a reasonable interpretation regarding the function of most of the rooms in Qumran.

The tower in the northwestern corner of the eastern building provided protection from attacks by nomads. From this tower one can see the western building, in which the hoard of silver coins, storehouses, a horse stable and millstones were discovered. As noted above, this building seems to have been the administrative center of the community.

Two of the inkwells found at Qumran.

In the eastern building, south of the tower, a room has been discovered with tables made of plaster. The longest table is about 5 meters long. Two small tables, with depressions in the plaster, look like writing desks. In this room, three inkwells have been found, two made of clay and one of bronze. A fourth inkwell, of clay, was found in the courtyard; it is situated in the middle of the eastern building and behind the eastern wall of this room. Since these tables were found in the debris, which fell from the upper floor, and one of the inkwells was found behind the wall of the lower room,

The "scriptorium" at the site.

Clay desks
(reconstructed)
from the
scriptorium,
shown here in
the Rockefeller
Museum.

one may conclude that the desks and the inkwells were used on the upper floor. This room perhaps served as the "scriptorium" in which some of the scrolls may have been copied.

The so-called "library" showing the window into the reading room.

West of the "scriptorium" is another room with low benches. De Vaux assumed that this was a classroom in which the members of the sect studied at night. He also posited that two rooms located south of this room, with wall shelves, served as the library.

South of the eastern structure was the dining room and a storeroom. Over one thousand clay vessels, arranged one inside the other, were discovered in the storeroom. These vessels may be divided into six categories. The majority consists of three kinds of personal eating utensils, and includes 708 deep bowls, 210 plates and 75 cups.

Father Milik in the storeroom with vessels in situ.

The other types of items comprise serving vessels, including 38 deep large bowls, 21 jars for liquids, and 11 jugs for the serving of warm drinks. Because the vessels were discovered in the storeroom, scholars concur that the large room near it was the sect's dining room. The size of this room and the number of the vessels indicate that the Qumran community included between 100 and 150 members. It seems that the people of Qumran had just finished cleaning and arranging the vessels when the earthquake of 31 BCE occurred, destroying the ceiling of the storeroom. After its destruction, the storeroom was not cleaned up, but a new floor was built over the broken vessels. In the course of this construction, hundreds of clay vessels were found between the two floors of this building.

A number of ritual baths are concentrated around the dining room. These pools are lined with watertight plaster and have wide steps leading to the floor of the pool. A feature characterizing the ritual baths in Qumran is a plaster line on the stairs, which separated between people entering and leaving the immersion pool. In certain baths there are two separating lines, and it seems that stepping into the area between the two lines was prohibited. In most baths, the separating lines do not divide the stairs into two equal parts but rather into a narrow and a wider part, one side being twice as wide as the other. It seems that the wider part served those who entered the bath and the narrow part served those coming out from the bath, suggesting that those who exited following immersion did so in single-file so as not to touch each other lest they were impure because of coming in touch

A ritual bath with two sets of staircases in the northern part of the site.

A ritual bath near the dining room. Note the "line" separating those entering and leaving the bath.

with a dead body and thus were not purified by the immersion. A person who came in touch with a dead body had to purify himself for a whole week and be sprinkled with purifying water.

The concentration of ritual baths near the dining room indicates that the Qumran residents used to bathe before the common meals. Their strict adherence to the act of purifying themselves before regular meals could be explained by assuming that the common meals in Qumran were a kind of substitute for the meals in the Jerusalem Temple in which the meat of the sacrifices was served. They seem to have avoided participation in the ceremonies at the Jeru-

The "dining room."

salem Temple because of their criticism of the priestly establishment of Jerusalem.

The reason for building over a dozen purification baths at the site seems to be the lack of rainfall. The aqueduct brought water only when floods filled Wadi Qumran and the water channels leading to the many pools served to utilize to the maximum the few occasions when rain fell and ensure that as little water as possible was wasted in natural runoff. It seems that the baths were used according to a certain plan, that is, the people of the Yahad community used a certain bath until the water became unclean and then switched to another bath. One may assume that when the water of all the baths became unclean, the entire group then went every day, before the common meal, to bathe in the springs of Ein Feshkha, about half an hour walking distance.

Bathers today in the waters of Ein Feshkha.

South of the dining room there is a large plateau. In the eastern section of this plateau a wall was built, separating it from the graveyard. Sect members likely used this area for prayer. Josephus noted that when the Essenes prayed, they turned to the east (*The Jewish War* II, 128), although the Holy Temple in Jerusalem, which was to the west of Qumran, was customarily faced in Jewish prayer throughout the country. Most of the scholars agree that the Qumran sect was one of the Essene groups, in which case it is reasonable to assume that the members of the sect gathered each morning before sunrise at the plateau, south of the site, and prayed while facing the rising sun. Each evening, after their common meal, they again gathered on the plateau, and recited the evening prayer while turning east, with their back to Jerusalem.

During the excavation season of 1955, Roland de Vaux noticed that in the southern corner of the plateau above Wadi Qumran there were stairs hewn in the marl terrace descending southward. These stairs led to three collapsed caves. In Cave 7, fragments of scrolls were found which contained four compositions in Greek: the Septuagint version of Exodus; a Greek translation of the Book of Enoch; and a number of unclassified fragments, identified by some scholars as parts of the New Testament Gospel of Mark and of the first epistle to Timothy. Although this identification is not convincing, it has raised great interest in these fragments. On the floor of Cave 7 blocks of marl were found which fell from the cave's ceiling and which bear Greek letters written in mirror image. These letters are the contact imprints of a text of a lost papyrus.

Fragment from Cave 7 which some scholars attempt to identify with the New Testament.

Imprints of papyrus fragments, from Cave 7.

Remains of leather straps for tying the scrolls.

This find indicates that the ceiling of Cave 7 collapsed after the rain fell at the site resulting in the ink being copied to the wet marl blocks. Since all the fragments from Cave 7 are in Greek, one may assume that the members who lived in Cave 7 read only Greek.

In a nearby cave, now designated as Cave 8, fragments of five compositions in Hebrew were found: a fragment of Genesis; fragments of the book of Psalms; a sheet of phylacteries; and a mezuzah. In addition, excavators found about one hundred square leather pieces with a notch in their center through which a narrow leather thong was drawn. One hundred similar square leather pieces were also found with scroll fragments in Cave 4a. In two cases, square pieces were found attached to the frontal page of leather scrolls (one of the manuscripts of the Damascus Document

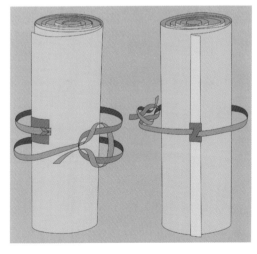

Tying of the scrolls.

Fragment of the prayer for the well-being of King Jonathan and (below) facsimile.

and the fragment of the prayer for the well-being of King Jonathan). After reading, the scroll was rolled back to its beginning and tied with the leather thong which was drawn into the square leather piece. It is possible that Cave 8 served as a workshop for the manufacture of these leather pieces, and its residents seem to have fixed a mezuzah at its entrance and brought to this cave phylacteries and some biblical scrolls.

In the third cave, designated as Cave 9, a single fragment has been found with the remains of three lines of an unidentified composition.

Most of the cooking pots at Khirbet Qum-

(above) Cave 9,
looking east.

Steps of the ritual
bath cracked in the
earthquake of 31
BCE.

ran were found in the central courtyard of the eastern building. Scholars agree that this was the area where food was cooked before being served in the common meals. In the courtyard one can observe a clear archaeological example of the damage caused to a building in the earthquake of 31 BCE. The eastern part of the stairs leading to the ritual bath built in this courtyard sank about 30 cm as a result of the quake, after which this bath ceased to be used.

About 100 meters east of the site is a cemetery with slightly more than 1,150 graves. One grave was excavated by Charles Clermont-Ganneau in 1873, and two others were excavated by G. L. Harding and de Vaux in 1949 during the preliminary stage of their archaeological research at Khirbet Qumran. Later, de Vaux excavated an additional 24 graves at this cemetery.

Charles Clermont-Ganneau.

A grave sealed with flat stones.

The graves in the Qumran cemetery are marked by stone heaps, most of which are arranged in a north-south direction. The bodies were buried in trenches 1.30 to 2 meters deep, either under the stone heaps or parallel to them. The trench was sealed with flat stones or bricks. According to de Vaux, the bodies were buried on their back, face up, with the hands parallel to the length of the body. Except for one grave, in which two skeletons were found together, each grave contained only one body. Almost no

Grave with the remains of a skeleton.

burial gifts were found in the graves. In one grave, a clay oil lamp was discovered. In another grave, a secondary burial of the bones of two bodies was discovered with the bones arranged in two separate groups. This indicates that they had been buried in another place and after their flesh withered away they were removed to the graveyard of Qumran. Fragments of a jug, similar to jugs found in the community center in phase Ib, were found in the earth covering this secondary burial. In the center of the

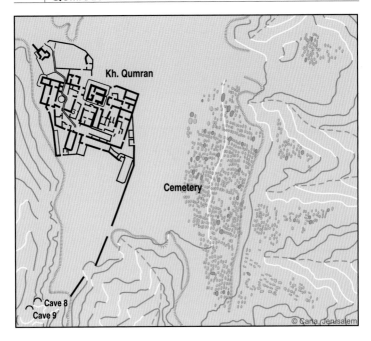

Plan of the cemetery, looking north.

cemetery were three graves containing the remains of three wooden coffins.

The graveyard extends over three hills on its east side. In this area, the orientation of some of the graves differs from that in the western part of the cemetery. Their orientation is east–west rather than north–south. Here, de Vaux excavated seven graves, finding in two of them evidence for secondary burials of two males, and in the remaining five graves the bodies of four women and of one child. The women were buried wearing their ornaments—beads and earrings. Recently it became clear that the beads found in these east–west oriented graves are characteristic of Bedouin graves. It seems that some of the burials

General view of the cemetery.

in this area are late. Recently nine more graves have been examined in this part of the cemetery. In two of them no skeletons have been found but rather jugs sealed with plaster covers dating from the Second Temple period.

In 1967, a scholar named Solomon H. Steckoll excavated nine more graves in the

The "mourning enclosure" and plan (below).

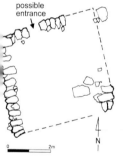

possible
entrance

0   2m

N

Qumran cemetery. In one of them the body of a sixty-five-year-old male was found. Most of the deceased buried in Qumran were much younger. In 2001, a number of graves were examined in the eastern part of the cemetery and remains of a zinc coffin were discovered. East of this grave, there are remains of a single room, classified as a "mourning room," in which possibly mourner's meals took place after burials. Under the floor of this room bones of two women (perhaps in secondary burial) were found dating from the Second Temple period. Under this room, excavations revealed the body of a thirty-year-old male. Near him was a cooking pot intact.

According to data gathered from various excavations in the cemetery, until now burial graves of two or three women and about thirty men from the Second Temple period have been uncovered. One has to emphasize the fact that the number of women buried in the cemetery is not proof that women actually lived in Qumran since the discovery of secondary burials in the graveyard east of the site indicates that some of the deceased were brought there from other places. It seems that some people considered it important to be buried in this cemetery. No doubt, among the disciples of the Teacher of Righteousness there were some women who lived according to the rules described in the Damascus Document. One may assume that a number of women lived in Qumran, helping with the work, which was considered women's work in the days of the Second Temple. It should be emphasized that the ratio of males to females in this cemetery completely differs from that found in all other Jewish cemeteries dating from the Second Temple period, in which the majority of the burials were women (about 60%). In any case, the number of female graves found in the cemetery east of Khirbet Qumran is too few on which to make an evaluation that women, indeed, lived at Qumran.

Cooking pot found underneath the floor of the "mourning enclosure."

Most of those buried here died young. For this fact two explanations have been offered: (1) hard conditions in the desert and an ascetic life; (2) members who survived were not able to continue living under these conditions and moved to other communities where conditions were better, but perhaps

Cave 10 (on the right) above Cave 4b.

Interior of Cave 4a.

maintained a way of life in accordance with the laws described in the Damascus Document. These two explanations do not contradict each other and both may be correct. Josephus, who had been a priest in Jerusalem, wrote in his autobiography that he left his home in Jerusalem at the age of 16 in order to learn about the religious sect active in his time. He joined a priest named Banus and stayed with him in the Judean desert for three years. At the age of 19 he returned to his family in Jerusalem. It is possible that Josephus was not exceptional in this. It seems that the Yahad sect appealed mainly to young people, mostly from priestly families, who were critical toward the Jerusalem authorities and who had a strong faith in God. They joined the sect, stayed there a few years, and after becoming less extreme in their beliefs, returned to their families.

In one of their visits to Cave 4a during 1955, the excavators noticed a mat covered with earth lying on the slope between Caves 4a and 4b. Removing the earth from the mat revealed that it lay on the floor of a cave most of which had been swept into Wadi Qumran. On the mat there was a decorated oil lamp and a fragment of a jug with two letters—*YŠ* [from the beginning of an inscription]. Although no scrolls were found in this cave, it was named Cave 10.

The finds from the artificial caves hewn in the marl rock near Qumran indicate that these caves were used for residential purposes. Other finds from the caves were cooking pots and storage vessels, as well as serving plates typical of an ordinary kitchen. The marl soil has forty percent water content and thus even the slightest wind makes residential conditions in the marl caves quite pleasant. This is the reason that most of these caves have more than one opening. Nowadays, even in the extreme heat of summer, staying in Cave 4a is pleasant. It would appear, then, that this primitive air-conditioning arrangement permitted desert dwellers to withstand the intense climatic conditions during the hot hours of summer days.

Remains of a mat found on the floor of a collapsed cave near Cave 9 during excavations in 2001.

Cave 11.

Cave 11

In January or February 1956, Bedouin of the Ta'amireh tribe again discovered an important cave. They noticed a bat coming out from a rift in the limestone cliff south of Cave 3, and discovered that this rift led to a cave sealed by a large rock. After moving the rock they were able to enter a large cave, which previously was not visible. Inside the now-designated Cave 11, thirty-one scrolls were found, four of them quite well preserved.

Following this discovery, the Jordanians again faced financial problems. Four scrolls from Cave 11 were quite long and over time the price of these scrolls increased. At this stage it was already clear that there was no guarantee that government or public institutions could afford to purchase the scrolls

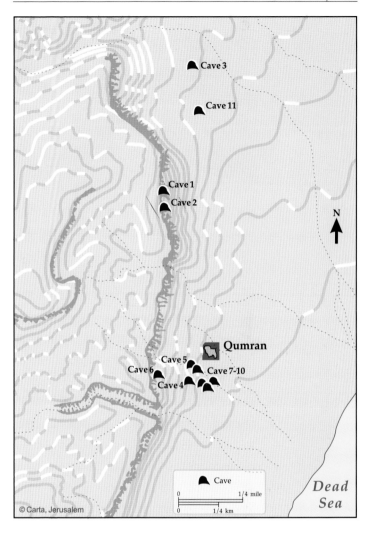

The Qumran caves and vicinity.

in order to keep them in their country out of Jordan. Since the Jordanians did not want to give up the scrolls and since the time required until their publication could not be predicted, they decided to finance the purchase of the scrolls from the Kingdom's budget, but delay opening the parchments and conducting research until the scholars

found funds for these activities. A decision was made that a scholar who wanted to publish the contents of the scrolls would pay the Jordanians the price the latter had paid to the Bedouin.

One of the most important findings in Cave 11 is the scroll of Leviticus written in Paleo-Hebrew script. It has survived in twelve fragmentary columns and contains parts of chapters 14–27. The importance of this scroll relates to the fact that there are three different versions of the Pentateuch: the Masoretic text, preserved by the Jews; the Greek version known as the Septuagint and preserved in the Christian Bible; and a Harmonistic version, held by the Samaritans, in which certain contradictions in the Pentateuch are explained away. The Leviticus scroll from Cave 11 displays an independent version, different from all three versions mentioned above. Therefore, one has to conclude that during the period of the Second Temple, the Jews were familiar

Prof. David Noel Freedman (1922–2008).

Detail of the Leviticus scroll from Cave 11.

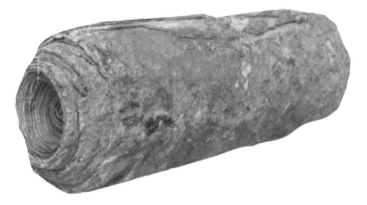

The unopened Psalms Scroll found in Cave 11.

with more than three versions of the Pentateuch (the Five Books of Moses). The Leviticus scroll from Cave 11 was entrusted to the biblical scholar, David Noel Freedman, for publication and was published by him and by his student, Kenneth Alan Mathews, in 1985.

Another well-preserved find from Cave 11 is the Psalms Scroll. This item includes thirty-six psalms from the Book of Psalms, arranged in a different order than that of the Masoretic text, together with eight hymns not included in the latter. Before being opened, the very-well preserved scroll

Detail of the Psalms Scroll.

looked like a large paper roll (some fragments of the scroll were bought together with the roll). This scroll was kept in the Rockefeller Museum until November 1961, when the American scholar James Sanders obtained the sum of money the Bedouin asked for it, thus acquiring the rights for its publication. The scroll is written on calf hide, a rare phenomenon among the Qumran scrolls, most of which were written on sheep, goat or ibex (mountain goat) hides. The copyist of the Psalms Scroll, which is written in the so-called "Jewish" script regularly, wrote the name of God in the Hebrew script. The different order of the psalms is explained by certain scholars as reflecting the work of a different editor of the Book of Psalms. Other scholars suggest that this scroll was used for prayer, and the different order reflects the order of the psalms as cited in the prayer services. The order of the psalms in the Masoretic text, as is well known, has been fixed according to the headings of the hymns, regardless of their nature and contents. Thus, all the hymns ascribed to Korah and to Asaph appear together, as do the hymns headed "Song of Ascents." Since the prayers are cited according to subjects, the order of the psalms in the Bible do not fit that of the prayer service and therefore they had to be arranged anew according to their contents. (This rearrangement is the basis for the term *Siddur* [prayer book], which derives from the Hebrew root *s-d-r*, "to arrange.") The hymns, which do not appear in the Masoretic text, are of special interest. Four

A column from the Psalms Scroll showing the correction (dots) above the name of God in Hebrew script.

Interior of Cave 11.

of these eight hymns were already known in Greek or Syrian translations. Now the Hebrew version of these hymns has been discovered. In a dozen Syriac manuscripts, the earliest dating from the eleventh century CE, five hymns appear which are not included in the Masoretic text. Three of these appear in the Psalms Scroll from Cave 11. In view of this fact, Sanders assumed that Timotheus I, the Patriarch of Seleucia in the late eighth and early ninth centuries, who asked for books which were found in a cave near Jericho and which included hymns unknown in the biblical version, received a scroll from Qumran which included five additional hymns, and in this way these hymns reached the Syriac version. The four hymns, unknown before the discovery of the scroll in Cave 11, are very interesting. Most beautiful is a Psalm for Zion, its verses being arranged alphabetically. Another text lists the compositions of King David, which, according to this list, number 364, a song for each day of the year, to be cited in front of the altar.

Most of the scrolls discovered in Cave 11 were bought by the Government of the Netherlands in 1961, for 10,000 pounds sterling. The Government decided to establish a center for Qumran research at

Entrance of Cave 11.

Fragment of the Targum (translation) of Job.

the University of Groningen, and as part of this project it acquired the publication rights to twenty-eight scrolls from Cave 11. The longest of these scrolls, from which thirty-eight columns survived, contained fragments from the Aramaic translation of the Book of Job (chs. 17–42). The Hebrew language of the Book of Job is quite difficult to understand, and therefore this was one of the first biblical books to be translated into Aramaic, the spoken tongue during the Second Temple period (fragments of the Aramaic translation of the Book of Job were also found in Cave 4). In the rabbinic works there is a story which indicates the existence of a translation of the Book of Job already in the time of the Second Temple, and certain sages tried to prohibit its reading in order to force the people to study the Hebrew version.

It is told of Rabbi Halafta that he went to visit Rabban Gamliel in Tiberias and found him sitting near the table of Johanan, son of Nazif, holding in his hand the Aramaic translation of the Book of Job, and he was reading it. Said to him Rabbi Halafta: I remember Rabban Gamliel the Elder, your grandfather, sitting on a step at the temple mount, and they brought before him the translated Book of Job. And he told the mason to secrete it under a course. Immediately Rabban Gamliel gave an order, and it (the translated book) was secreted.

Tosefta, *Shabbat* 13,2–3; BT, *Shabbat* 115a; JT, *Shabbat* 16,1; 15,73

Facsimile of one fragment of the Targum of Job.

This story tells of Rabban Gamliel of the Jabneh generation, who lived after the destruction of the Second Temple. It may be assumed that the version of the translation brought to his grandfather the Elder Rabban Gamliel resembled that found in Cave 11 at Qumran,.

Another important scroll bought by the Netherlands government deals with Melchizedek. This scroll is one of the most interesting sectarian scrolls found in Qumran, since its composer interpreted in an original way verses extracted from different biblical books. For example, he claimed that the commands concerning the Sabbatical and Jubilee years do not refer to the waiver of money debts and return of the real estate but, in fact, deal with the spiritual repent. This scroll is important because of the role of Melchizedek in Hebrews 7 in the New Testament.

In Cave 11, Bedouin found the longest

scroll discovered in Qumran—the Temple Scroll (8.30 m). Kando, again acting as middleman between the Bedouin and the Rockefeller Museum, estimated that this deal would bring him a handsome fortune, and set a price of one million dollars for its purchase. He therefore decided not to deliver it to the Museum and hid the scroll under the floor of his home in Bethlehem. He thought that scholars would not invest such huge sums of money for an object that was of uncertain legal status. Assuming that the

The Temple Scroll.

Jordanian government, which refused to accept the existence of the Jewish state, would not sue an Israeli citizen, he tried to sell the scroll to Yigael Yadin, who had already acquired scrolls in the past. He asked an American Protestant pastor named Joseph (Joe) Uhrig, from Virginia, to be the middleman between him and Yadin. During the negotiations, Yadin examined two fragments of the Temple Scroll and in 1961 he paid ten thousand dollars for the scroll. However, he received neither the scroll nor

Detail of the Temple Scroll.

the money in return. Only six years later, after the Israeli army conquered Bethlehem in the Six-Day War, did Yadin, who served as the military adviser for Prime Minister Levi Eshkol, ask military intelligence to search Kando's house and find the scroll. Indeed, the Temple Scroll was found under the floor of his house; in the course of the eleven years it lay hidden, more damage was caused to the scroll than had occurred during the 1,900 years it was hidden in Cave 11, all its upper part having rotted. After the war, the Israeli government paid Kando 125,000 dollars for the Temple Scroll.

The unopened Temple Scroll.

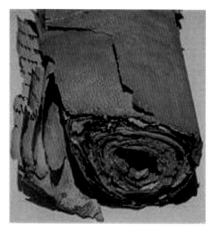

The Temple Scroll differs in some aspects from the other sectarian scrolls. Thus, it lists in detail the rules for the management of the Temple, unlike the other scrolls which only show expectations that the

Temple be managed by members of the Yahad sect. Also unlike the other scrolls, it does not criticize the Hasmonean kings but only lists rules referring to the king. Therefore, scholars are divided over the question whether the composer of the Temple Scroll belonged to the Yahad sect and whether the scroll had been composed before the sect went to dwell in the Judean desert. Some scholars think that the Temple Scroll origi-

Reconstruction of the Temple court in Jerusalem according to the Temple Scroll.

nated with another group of dissidents from Jerusalem, whose views were similar but not identical with those of the Yahad group.

After 1956, no additional scrolls were found in Qumran. The fragments of about nine hundred scrolls were found in eleven different caves in Qumran between 1947 and 1954. Five of these (Caves 1, 2, 3, 6 and 11) are natural caves, formed in the limestone, and the remaining six (Caves 4, 5, 7–10) are artificial caves, carved in the marl stone.

A Visit to Qumran

Most visitors drive their vehicles directly to the national park at Khirbet Qumran. A recommended, but longer route is to turn west from the main road as you approach the national park. Instead of climbing the hill to the site, drive on an inner road northward, toward Kibbutz Kalya. About 200 m from the junction of the road ascending to the visitors' center and the inner road, there is a small tamarisk grove on the west side of the road. This grove was planted by Roland de Vaux and marks the closest that cars can come to the first cave, discovered by the Bedouin in 1947. This cave (Cave 1) is located in the lower third of the cliff. Its openings cannot be seen from the grove, since they face one of the clefts on the southern slope. In order to see Cave

Coins found in the excavations at Khirbet Qumran.

1, one has to climb up to it. However, Cave 2 may be seen from the grove.

Cave 2 (entrance indicated by red arrow).

After reaching Kibbutz Kalya, continue north on a well-trodden dirt road. After about 400 m, the road reaches a fence that encircles residential neighborhood build-

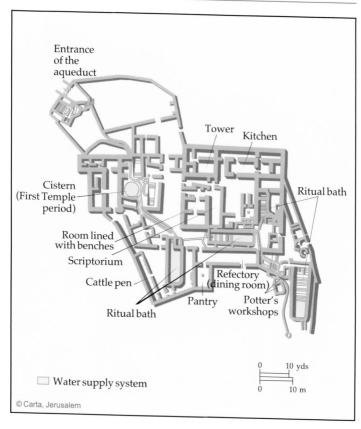

Plan of Khirbet Qumran.

ings near Kalya. At the end of this fence is a small parking area to the east of the road (right-hand side, facing north). Looking west towards the cliff, one can see the trapezoidal opening of Cave 11, on the lower third of the cliff. A path leads to the cave. Cave 11 is one of the most important found at Qumran (together with Caves 1 and 4). As in Cave 1, Cave 11 yielded four scrolls in good condition (see above). This is one of the two caves located far to the north, about three kilometers from Khirbet Qumran. About half a kilometer north of Cave

11 is Cave 3, where the Copper Scroll was discovered.

The twin caves excavated by Vendyl Jones.

To the south of Cave 11, two openings of caves, side-by-side, may be observed, as well as a garbage dump below. These "twin caves" were excavated by Pessah Bar-Adon, who hoped to find here one of the treasures mentioned in the Copper Scroll. The sixth column of the scroll describes a treasure which was hidden in "the cave of the column of the two openings." According to this description, an additional copy of the scroll had been hidden in the northern opening of the cave, as well as twenty-two talents of silver and a *qalal*—a big goblet with a broad edge, mostly made of stone. This type of goblet was used in the Jerusalem Temple to keep the ashes of the red heifer. During his excavations, Bar-Adon met an

Large limestone goblet found in Ein Feshkha reminiscent of the qalal mentioned in the Copper Scroll.

Clay vessels found north of Khirbet Qumran in the winter of 1996.

American priest named Vendyl Jones, who was convinced that the treasures of the Temple were hidden in this cave. After Bar-Adon's death in 1985, Jones continued his excavations in the cave under the supervision of Joseph Patrich and other scholars. However, no treasure has been discovered in the two caves despite the huge amounts of earth removed.

Return from this place to the car park at the entrance to the national park of Khirbet Qumran. Most visitors to the site begin their visit watching an eight-minute film, which renders basic information concerning the sect and its relation to early Christianity. From the film room, proceed to a small exhibit displayed in the adjoining three rooms. At the entrance to the exhibit is a triangular room illustrating Cave 1 as seen by Muhammad ed-Dibb when he entered it in the summer of 1947. Note the replications of

Muhammad ed-Dibb in later years.

the cylindrical jugs that were found in the cave.

Near the triangular room is a model of a ritual bath with two citations from the scrolls concerning purification rules observed by the Qumran community. The next room is dedicated to the common meal, with replicas of clay vessels placed in the storeroom. A large stone vessel in the form of a big goblet, identified by most scholars as a *qalal* (see above), stands near the vessels.

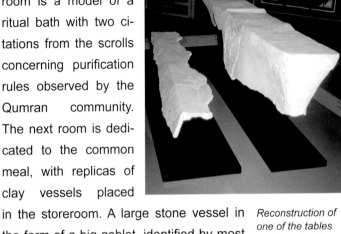

Reconstruction of one of the tables and benches from the Scriptorium.

The last room in the exhibit is devoted to the scrolls. It contains a copy of the Scroll of the Community Rule and a replica of one of the plaster tables found in the "scriptorium." A number of artifacts from the excavations in Qumran are displayed opposite

End fragment of the Community Rule scroll.

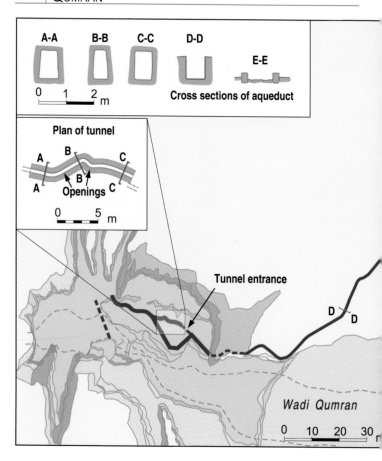

A-A B-B C-C D-D

E-E

0 1 2 m

Cross sections of aqueduct

Plan of tunnel

A B C

B

A **Openings** C

0 5 m

Tunnel entrance

D D

Wadi Qumran

0 10 20 30 m

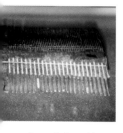

A comb found in Khirbet Qumran.

the door leading from the exhibit to the site (a broken comb, remains of sandals, torn baskets, ropes, and a fragment of a stone vessel). The other articles on display are replicas.

On entering the site, it is best to enter the sunscreen shed north of the archaeological remains. From there one can view the five natural caves in the limestone cliff where the scrolls were discovered. Farther north, beyond the modern pool of Kibbutz Kalya, is the region of Caves 3 and 11. In the cen-

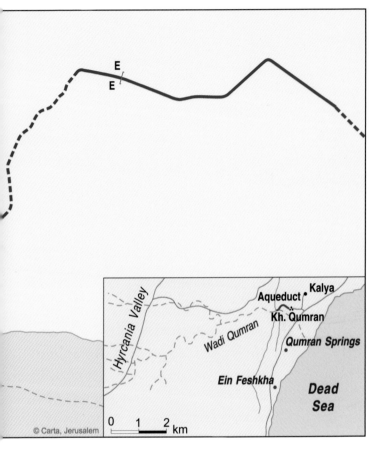

E
E

Hyrcania Valley

Aqueduct • Kalya

Kh. Qumran

Wadi Qumran

Qumran Springs

Ein Feshkha •

Dead Sea

© Carta, Jerusalem

0 1 2 km

Plan of the aqueduct.

tral cliff are Caves 1 and 2, and opposite Qumran, to the right of the green sign of the Nature Reserves Authority below the cliff, is Cave 6. The caves in the marl rock will be viewed at a later stage of the visit.

From the shed, it is possible to walk westward to the cliff faults, toward the green sign to the west of the site at the base of the cliff. During the walk the aqueduct can be seen on the left—an open canal to the north of the path. On reaching the green sign, the marked path turns south. Imme-

View of the aqueduct, with the Dead Sea and Moab Mountains in background.

diately, a cave with a triangular opening comes into view. This is Cave 6, in which the Bedouin found fragments from thirty-one different scrolls, most of them written on papyrus. Farther south, the path reaches Wadi Qumran, that is, the riverbed. The four waterfalls of the wadi are dry most of the year, with water flowing only during flash floods. The marked path leads to the region between the second and third waterfalls. Sit down above the third waterfall and look to the east, to the ruins of Qumran and to the Dead Sea. From this place, an artificial cave with a triangular opening in the marl rock may be clearly viewed. This is Cave 4b.

At this stage, one may climb up the stream to the bottom of the second waterfall. In this region, a big dam, which diverted part of

(above) Caves 4b (on the left) and 10.

(left) The view of Wadi Qumran from the western opening of Cave 4b.

Remains of the dam below the waterfall in Wadi Qumran.

Nails dating from the Second Temple period found on the path north of the aqueduct built on the marl terrace.

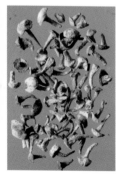

the floodwaters into the aqueduct, was built during the Second Temple period. This dam is mentioned in the Copper Scroll as "the large stone pile in the Secacah stream." The location of the dam below the falls is reasonable, since after falling into the pool the reduced waterpower is less likely to ruin the dam. North of the waterfall, carved into the rock, is the aqueduct. The aqueduct enters a hewn tunnel. Visitors may crawl inside. From the tunnel, one returns to the marked path, which leads back to Khirbet Qumran.

On reaching the site, it is recommended first to climb to the top of the tower, in order to view the archaeological remains. This is a suitable place for a discussion of the archaeological history of the site.

The aqueduct and entrance (close-up view below) into the hewn tunnel in the cliff.

As mentioned above, Qumran existed during the Iron Age II and was occupied from the late eighth century BCE until shortly before the destruction of the First Temple by the Babylonians in 586 BCE. From this period are the remains of the round water cistern located in the western part of the site. After a long gap during which the site was abandoned, settlement was renewed, perhaps towards the end of the second century or the beginning of

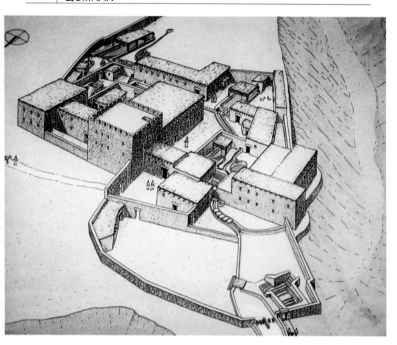

Reconstruction of Khirbet Qumran.

the first century BCE. The site was destroyed by a powerful earthquake in 31 BCE, rebuilt after the quake and destroyed again during the turmoil in Judea after Herod's death in 4 BCE. It was restored soon afterwards and destroyed by the Roman army in 68 CE. A Roman military force occupied Qumran until the fall of Masada in the spring of 73 or 74 CE. Afterwards the site was abandoned and never settled again. A group of Jewish rebels used the destroyed tower to oversee the northern part of the Dead Sea at the end of the Bar Kokhba revolt (132–136 CE). During the excavations conducted by Roland de Vaux, an oil lamp containing a number of coins from the time of Bar Kokhba's revolt was found at the top of the tower.

Jug that contained one third of the silver hoard found in the western structure.

As already noted, no scrolls were found inside the ruins, and the assumptions concerning the function of the different rooms at the site are based on certain considerations which combine archaeological data and textual clues in the texts and in the writings of Josephus Flavius.

From the tower it is easy to see that Qumran is divided into an eastern structure and a western structure built around the round water cistern. The western structure possibly served administrative purposes. In it were stored the community's food supplies. Three jugs, filled with purposely-hidden silver coins, were found under the floor of one of the storage rooms. Also found in the western structure were basalt-stone grinding implements, called "donkey's millstones" in the Rabbinic sources, since they were operated by donkeys or by mules.

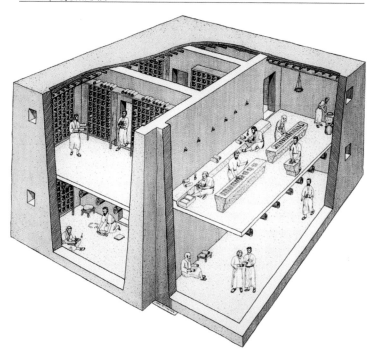

Reconstruction of the Scriptorium.

Near the western structure, a stable was built for the mules, which carried water from Ein Feshkha to Qumran.

The eastern structure possibly served as the community center, since it seems that its rooms were used by the entire group and not only for administrative personnel. Descending from the tower, enter the "scriptorium" (room 30). While walking through the corridor leading to this room, note the remains of stairs at the southern (right) section of the corridor. These stairs led to the second floor. In the "scriptorium," plaster benches, together with three inkwells, were found. Another inkwell was found near this room, beyond its eastern wall. Plaster tables were found in the debris that had fallen from the second floor. Since long tables did not serve for writing in the time of the Second Temple, nor was their design suitable for writing comfortably, scholars now concur that these tables were used for preparing the scrolls and for their unrolling, as well as for marking the columns and the lines. It would appear, then, that scribal activity, including the preparation of the scrolls, took place on the second floor of this structure.

Additional evidence for the activity of scribes in Qumran is an ostracon (broken clay sherds were used as cheaply available writing material) on which a scribe wrote the letters of the alphabet, perhaps as a scribal exercise. This ostracon was found near the sunscreen shelter, north of the site.

A clay inkwell (top) and a bronze inkwell (above) found in the Scriptorium.

Leaving the "scriptorium," enter the nearby room (room 4), which contains low

Scribal exercise on a pottery sherd, found north of the site.

Study room (room no. 4) lined with benches.

plaster benches attached to its walls. The plaster floors consist of a number of layers, one above the other. The inner rooms were paved with pebbles. Near the entrance to the room with the benches is a plastered installation built into the wall. A pipe, which begins outside the door, joins this installation. Between this room and the two inner rooms, there are three "windows" (two of them are now open, whereas the third is blocked-up by earth). It is unclear if these "windows" were once openings between the two rooms or perhaps were wooden wall cupboards. In the room where the benches are located, de Vaux found a number of oil lamps. Based on the findings of the plaster benches, the "windows" which join the two rooms, and the oil lamps, de Vaux concluded that the room with the benches served

Oil lamps found at the site.

the people of Qumran for their nightly studies. He assumed that part of the scrolls were kept in the two inner rooms, and that the "windows" between the rooms were used to pass the scrolls from the "library" to the readers, or as shelves for the scrolls.

As noted above, Khirbet Qumran was destroyed three times: in 31 BCE, in 4 BCE and in 68 CE. Each time the destruction was accompanied by fire. In the Second Temple period, it was more convenient to keep fire burning during the day than lighting it anew

Installation built into the wall of the "study room."

every evening. This practice meant that the destruction of ceilings, whatever the cause, usually caused fires, even if it occurred during daylight hours. The structures at Qumran were covered with wooden beams made of the trunks of palm trees (usually cut into halves) on which palm branches were spread, as well as mats (this practice seems to be reflected in the ancient name of the site Secacah). These roofs became dry in the sun and could easily catch fire. An enemy shooting a single flamed arrow could easily have caused the entire site to be fire-gutted. The bad experience of the Qumran people was perhaps the reason that they decided to keep the scrolls in the caves rather than in the buildings. Even if a cave collapsed, there was little danger that it would catch fire, and the precious scrolls could be unearthed. That most of

Interior of Cave 4a, where most of the Dead Sea Scrolls may have been kept.

the scrolls from Qumran were kept in Cave *Cave 4 and surroundings.*
4a provides some basis for this assump-
tion. When this cave was full and no more
scrolls could be kept in it, the new scrolls
were placed in Cave 5. This assumption
could also explain why most of the scrolls
in Cave 4 are earlier (that is, copied at a
relatively earlier stage) than those in Cave
5. If this conjecture is correct, the people of
Qumran seem to have avoided keeping the
scrolls in the rooms built at the site because
of the danger of fire. Hence, if de Vaux was
right in postulating that the room with the
windows was a study room, the two rooms
found south of the room with the benches
would have contained only a small number
of scrolls for use during the regular nightly
study hours.

Walk south from this part of the structure,

The ritual bath north of the dining room.

pass through the corridor, which separates the western and the eastern parts of the site, and enter the dining room. Three large ritual baths are located close by. The steps leading down to the bath north of the dining room are divided by lines of plaster, marking the separation between the people who enter the bath and those leaving it. In this case, there are two separating lines. It seems that stepping in the area between the two lines was prohibited. The lines divide the stairs into two unequal parts, one twice as wide as the other. The wide part probably served those who entered the bath. Such a division is mentioned in the Mishna, which says that vessels found along the descent to the bath were unclean while the ones found along the ascent were pure (*Sheqalim* 8:2). An apocryphal Greek Gospel, found in Egypt, which describes the life of Jesus, tells that a Pharisaic high priest told Jesus that he descended into the purifying bath one way and came out another.

From the ritual bath one can enter the western part of the dining room. Another option is to take the wooden path, which crosses the site and first view the dining room from without. In view of evidence from the Manual of Discipline scroll, the seat of the priest who said the blessing over the bread and wine before the meal was at one of the narrow ends of the dining room. It is unclear if the diners were sitting in this room in three or in four rows. The size of the room indicates that the number of members in the group residing in Qumran was no more than 150, including the candidates and the unclean, who did not eat together with the other members.

South of the dining room is the pantry,

The dining room, looking southeast.

Some of the vessels found in the pantry.

where the dining vessels were kept for the common meals. In the center of the room, a base of a square column, which supported the ceiling, may be seen. The danger of hundreds of clay vessels being shattered by a collapsing ceiling seems to have been the reason for constructing this support column. However, this support did not save the many clay vessels kept in this room during the earthquake of 31 BCE. On the floor of this room, 708 deep bowls, 210 flat plates, and 75 cups were found. The vessels in which the food was served included 38 deep, large bowls; 21 jugs for containing liquids, such as water or wine; and 11 decanters, which were used for hot drinks. The dozens of personal vessels were found in heaps, piled one on top of the other.

The common meal, which took place daily in the afternoon hours, was the most important event of the day for the Qumran community. These repasts seem to have been of extended duration. During the meal, members drank wine (as evidenced in the Community Rule scroll), water, and a warm beverage—perhaps a concoction made of a certain plant growing near Qumran. The drinks were brought to the table in decanters. This hypothesis explains the large number of bowls found in the pantry, bowls that apparently also served for consuming the various drinks. It seems that in matters concerning meals and their duration, the people of Qumran were directly influenced by the practice at the Temple in Jerusalem and, indirectly, from the meals of the Greeks which also lasted a long time and in which various kinds of beverages were served.

The "pantry" with remains of the support column at its center.

South of the dining room is a stone-paved surface. At its eastern end there is an installation resembling a winepress. In the 1993 excavations at Qumran, about 100,000 date-pits were discovered. Similar presses for wine or honey produced from dates have been discovered in Jericho and Ein Feshkha.

To the south of this area, where wine and date-honey is manufactured, is a plateau reachable only through the site. Between this plateau and the cemetery east of the site was a stone wall. It seems that this plateau served the Qumran people as a place of prayer. Walking along the

(opposite) The "date press" on the plateau used to produce date wine and date honey.

Remains of dates and pits and the site of discovery (bottom).

(opposite) Close-up view of the eastern opening of Cave 4a.

western edge of this plateau one arrives at two huts from which Cave 4a may be seen. The entrance to this cave is through a passageway (serving like a stairway) carved in the marl rock and descending to the cave from the north. In Cave 4a, there are three windows opening towards Wadi Qumran. From the plateau the eastern window may be seen and, at a certain angle, the western window may also be seen through it. When reaching the southwestern end of the plateau, the terrace and the southern window of Cave 4a may be seen. As mentioned, about 16,000 scroll fragments were found

Interior of Cave 4a. The southern opening on the left leads to the terrace.

Scroll jar from the site of Khirbet Qumran.

in this cave. Certain scholars assume that a Roman soldier caused the first damage to these scrolls, and the rest was caused by insects and by harsh weather conditions. As stated above, this cave probably served as the "bookstore" of the people of Qumran, i.e., here they kept most of their scrolls.

After observing Cave 4a, continue to the southwestern edge of the plateau and look in the direction of Cave 5, located north of Cave 4a, at the northern end of the marl rock. The opening of this cave faces south. One may assume that when Cave 4a was filled to capacity with scrolls, additional scrolls were then stored in Cave 5. There-

Cave 5 with Khirbet Qumran in background.

fore, most of the scrolls found in Cave 4 were dated earlier than those found in Cave 5. It seems that when the Roman army approached Qumran in 68 CE, the members of the sect decided to move their scrolls to the natural caves hidden in the limestone cliff, located west of Qumran. They managed to transfer scrolls to Caves 1, 2, 3, 11 and 6, but were unable to finish this task and many scrolls remained in Caves 4a and 5. The fact that most of the scrolls in Cave 1 were mainly early copies, that is, they were copied at a relatively early stage, could be explained by suggesting that these scrolls were brought there from Cave 4, whereas most of the scrolls found in Cave 11 were later copies, possibly brought there from Cave 5.

Photos and drawing of the Hebrew ostracon found east of the wall separating the plateau from the cemetery. Note the actual size of the upper half (above).

Bulldozer used to dig the plateau.

After observing Cave 5, continue in an easterly direction towards the wall bordering the plateau on the east. Walk north along this wall and pass through an opening in the wall. East of the wall, where it continues to the north and northeast of the huts, there is a view of Cave 4a.

In 1996, an ostracon was discovered east of the wall separating the plateau from the cemetery. It bears 18 lines of writing in the so-called "Jewish" script of the first century CE. This text seems to be a deed of gift written in Hebrew and dated to year 2 based on an unnamed system of counting. According to this text, a person named Honi gave property of considerable value to a person

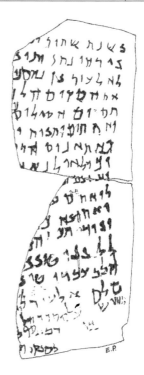

named Elazar, son of Nahmani. This property included a house as well as olive and fig trees. The Community Rule states that a candidate beginning his second year had to deliver all his property to the overseer and the latter had to write him an "account." In case the candidate was not received as a member of the sect, or if he decided to leave the sect during the second year, his property was returned to him. The scholars who published this text assumed that this was such an account, written by the overseer Elazar son of Nahmani for Honi, who wanted to become a member of the sect.

From this point, continue north until reaching the southeastern part of the communal

Potter's kiln.

Jug found in the wall of the kiln at Khirbet Qumran.

center. This area boasts a number of huge ritual baths, as well as a kiln for clay vessels. The presence of this kiln and another one, which no longer exists, suggests that a large center for the production of clay vessels existed in Qumran. This assumption is highly conjectural, since no clay suitable for such manufacture may be found at the site and, in addition, there is not enough kindling material to feed such kilns. Examination of the Qumran clay vessels and their chemical composition indicates that they came from a geological layer called "Motza marl," found in the Jerusalem region. Therefore, one may conclude that the people of Qumran brought a limited amount of clay from Jerusalem, and that the production of clay vessels in Qumran was undertaken not for

Ritual bath in the northern part of the site.

industrial but for purity reasons, that is, to assure that the vessels were acceptable according to the ritual laws.

From the potter's kiln continue walking northwest until reaching a courtyard, which was at the center of the eastern building. In this place stands the ritual bath, which had been damaged in the earthquake of 31 BCE. Apparently, the food for the common meals

(above) General view of the cemetery and (right) entrance to one of the graves.

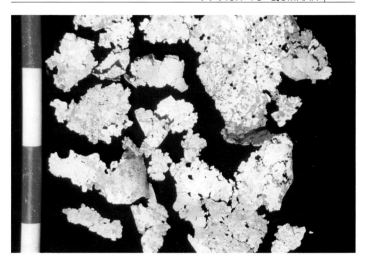

Fragments of the zinc coffin found in the "mourning enclosure."

was prepared in this courtyard. After looking at the damaged ritual bath turn east, exit the ruins of the buildings, and go to the cemetery located east of Khirbet Qumran. The southern section of the cemetery is its best-preserved area. The cemetery contains about 1,150 graves. Burial practice in Qumran was very different from that discovered in family burials in other places in Judea, including Jericho and Ein Gedi. The individual burial practiced in Qumran, and the absence of burial gifts in the graves, reflects the ideology of the members of the sect. Some scholars suggest that in the Second Temple period individual burial in simple trenches was typical of poor people. If this is correct, it would be interesting to learn that the Qumran people chose this kind of burial for themselves despite their wealthy background, originating in the upper classes of Judea.

Aerial view of Qumran, looking west.

Summary

The question may be raised how the people of Qumran succeeded in preserving the Messianic enthusiasm within the group during a period of almost two hundred years. The Commentaries (*Pesharim*) and the Damascus Document, which include details about the history of the sect, reflect a large number of disputes among the members and the withdrawal of disap-

pointed members from the Yahad community who were waiting in vain for the long expected redemption. These compositions tried to explain the delay of the redemption and, in order to encourage the members, promised it would come soon. There is no doubt that the fact that this group was wealthy and financially secure, helped it to survive these crises, including the disputes among the disciples of the Teacher of Righteousness. A substantial number of mem-

"4Q Testimonia," from Cave 4, a text which alludes to John Hyrcanus (134–104 BCE). The name "Testimonia" comes from an early type of Christian writing, which it resembles in literary style. The Christian Testimonia was a collection of verses from the Bible about the Messiah, strung together to prove some kind of point. The Testimonia from Qumran is not a Christian document, but does resemble the early Christian Testimonia because of its use of a number of verses dealing with a theme.

bers were priests, some from the house of Zadok—the family holding the office of the High Priesthood until it was taken by the Hasmonean dynasty. One may assume that the Zadokites belonged to the wealthy families in Jerusalem. Most members of the sect were learned people who gave up the pleasures of life in the upper city of Jerusalem to go to the desert. The idea of sharing property among the members of the sect developed in all probability as a reaction to the chasing of wealth among the Jerusalem priests. The life in Qumran was hard, and some of the members could not withstand these harsh conditions for long, and they left the group and returned to Jerusalem.

The scrolls found in Qumran testify not only to the lifestyle of the sect, but also to their dispute with the Pharisees, and to the halakhic views of the latter. In addition to the sectarian works, many other compositions have been discovered in Qumran not composed by the members of the sect. Among them are apocryphal psalms and works based on biblical stories, as well as various prayers, all testifying to the Jewish literary works in the time of the Second Temple. The Commentaries contain clues to political events taking place in Jerusalem and so far unknown details of the history of Judea in the Hasmonean period.

Despite being a small group of about 100 to 150 members, the Qumran sect has had an influence on western culture, that is, Judaism and Christianity. There is a certain affinity between some of Jesus' sermons (mainly the Sermon on the Mount in Matthew 5), and certain texts in the scrolls, mainly in the Thanksgiving Scroll. It also seems that in his letters Paul cited sectarian texts composed by members of the Yahad sect. Certain scholars investigating the scrolls are of the opinion that the composer of the Gospel According to St. John, who lived in Asia Minor, belonged to a congregation whose ideas resembled those of the Qumran sect. There are clear affinities between the early Jerusalem church, which is described in the Acts of the Apostles, and

Coin of Herod Antipas (4 BCE–39 CE).

the Qumran sect—for example, the sharing of property, the common meals, the overseer's office (called Episcopus in the early church), praying while facing east, and more. Certain scholars conjecture that both leaders of the early Jerusalem church, that is, Peter and James, the brother of Jesus, learned these practices from the disciples of John the Baptist, who was active in the vicinity of Qumran. John the Baptist was executed by Herod Antipas in 29 CE, a year before Jesus' crucifixion. There seems to be little doubt that some of the disciples of John the Baptist joined the disciples of Jesus after the execution of their teacher. They seem to have taught the leaders of the early Jerusalem church certain customs practiced by groups who left Jerusalem, such as the people of Qumran.

One should emphasize the fact that there is a significant difference between the public addressed by the Teacher of Righteousness, acting in the second century BCE, and the public addressed by Jesus, acting in the first century CE. Jesus addressed farmers and fishermen in the Galilee, seemingly illiterate and probably understanding only Aramaic, whereas the Teacher of Righteousness was the leader of a group consisting mostly of people belonging to the noble and rich priestly families from Jerusalem. All the members of his movement knew not only Aramaic but also Hebrew (and some also

Greek), but were also capable of spending a third of every night of the year reading the scrolls.

The ruins of Khirbet Qumran. On far left is the Scriptorium, and, to its right, the "study room" with the so-called "window" into the library.

The people of Qumran, or related groups, influenced Judaism after the destruction of the Second Temple. One of the institutions evolving with the groups who left Jerusalem in the time of the Second Temple was the fixed prayer, that is, a fixed text of the prayer to be cited at regular hours. This fixed prayer was not practiced by the Jews participating in the religious worship at the Temple in Jerusalem. Only after the destruction of the Temple was the fixed prayer adopted by the Sages, who turned it into the main religious practice of Jewish life, thus enabling the adaptation of the Jews to the new reality, a reality without a central sanctuary of worship.

If one of us would have met a member of the Qumran community before its destruc-

Kh. Qumran

Panoramic view of the site from above the third waterfall in Wadi Qumran, with the Dead Sea and Moab Mountains in the background.

tion by the Roman army in 68 CE, the latter would probably have told him that the group failed, because for two hundred years they waited, expecting their redemption and believing that they will soon become the leaders of the Jewish people and of the entire world, but this did not happen. However, two thousand years later, it seems not to have been a failure, since the people of Qumran influenced both Judaism and Christianity. From the scrolls one learns that the Yahad people made an important contribution to

Cave 4b

the formation of western culture, which developed in the wake of the destruction of the Second Temple. The influence of the Qumran people on the Jewish and Christian religions has not been documented in history books. The nine hundred scroll fragments discovered between 1947 and 1956 have revealed only the existence of this marvelous group of people, who gave up their comfortable way of life in Jerusalem to live a religious way of life in the desert consonant with their faith.

Select Bibliography

Cross, F. M., *The Ancient Library of Qumran*, 3rd edition, Minneapolis 1995.

Davies, P. R., G. J. Brooke and P. R. Callaway, *The Complete World of the Dead Sea Scrolls,* London 2002.

Eshel, H., *The Dead Sea Scrolls and the Hasmonean State,* Grand Rapids 2008.

Milik, J. T., *Ten Years of Discovery in the Wilderness of Judaea*, trsl. J. Strugnell, London 1959.

Schiffman, L. H., *Reclaiming the Dead Sea Scrolls,* Philadelphia 1994.

VanderKam, J. C., *The Dead Sea Scrolls Today*, Grand Rapids 1994.

VanderKam, J. C., and P. Flint, *The Meaning of the Dead Sea Scrolls,* New York 2002.

Vermes, *An Introduction to the Complete Dead Sea Scrolls,* London 1997.

Picture Sources

Index